The Book of Giants

By

W. B. Henning

ISBN: 978-1-63923-497-4

Printed: November 2022

Cover Art By: Amit Paul

Published and Distributed By:
Lushena Books
607 Country Club Drive, Unit E
Bensenville, IL 60106
www.lushenabks.com

ISBN: 978-1-63923-497-4

The Book of Giants

The Fallen Angels and their Giant Sons

By

W. B. Henning

PUBLISHER'S PREFACE

About the Book

"Ogias the Giant, also known as The Book of Giants is one of the books from the New Testament apocrypha which concerned the Old Testament. The text relates how before the great flood, there was a giant named Ogias who fought a great dragon. A brief mention of this giant, "Ohia" is found in the Babylonian Talmud (Nidah, Ch 9), where it is said "Sihon and Og [from the book of Genesis] were brothers, as they were the sons of Ohia the son of Semjâzâ [one of the leaders of the fallen angels in the Book of Enoch]".

The book is thought to have been based on the Book of Enoch, itself based on an obscure passage from Genesis (6:1-4) concerning Nephilim, which became "fallen angels". The book concerns itself with filling in the details about the giants and their offspring that the book of Enoch misses out. Aramaic fragments of it, along with other fragments of the Book of Enoch, were found among the Dead Sea Scrolls at Qumran. In the version of the Book of Giants which was spread by the Manichaean religion, the book became well travelled, and exists in Syriac, Greek, Persian, Sogdian, Uyghur, and Arabic, although each version is somewhat distorted, incorporating more local myths.

The version found at Qumran also describes the hero Gilgamesh and the monster Humbaba as two of the giants accompanying Ogias.

Its discovery at Qumran puts its date as at least before the 2nd century BC."

(Quote from wikipedia.org)

About the Author

W. B. Henning (1908 - 1967)

"Walter Bruno Henning (August 26, 1908 in Ragnit, Eastern Prussia – January 8, 1967 in Berkeley, California, United States) was a German-born scholar of Iranian history, noted for his contribution to the Middle Iranian corpus and the breadth of his interests, especially those subjects related to the wealth of archaeological discovery in the East Turkestan regions of China in the early 20th century."

(Quote from wikipedia.org)

CONTENTS

INTRODUCTION

I SAAC DE BEAUSOBRE, the Huguenot author of one of the best books ever written on Manichæism (Histoire critique de Manichée et du Manicheïsme, Amsterdam, 1734, 1739), was the one to make the only sound suggestions on the sources used by Mani for the compilation of his Book of the Giants: the Book of Enoch, and the Γραφὴ τῶν Γιγάντων which Kenan, a great-grandson of Noah, discovered lying in a field (vol. i, 429, n. 6). The latter work has been identified by Alfaric (Les Écritures Manichéennes, ii, 32) with a book whose contents are briefly indicated in the Decretum Gelasianum, p. 54, ll. 298-9 (ed. Dobschütz): Liber de Ogia[1] nomine gigante qui post diluvium cum dracone ab hereticis pugnasse perhibetur apocryphus. Of the Book of Enoch, which was composed in the Hebrew language in the second century B.C., only an Ethiopic version, a few Greek fragments, and some excerpts made by the Byzantine chronographer Georgius Syncellus survive.[2] Mani, who could hardly read the Hebrew, must have used an Aramaic edition based directly on the Hebrew text (see below, Šhmyz'd). He quotes mainly from the first part, which Georgius S. (p. 45, Fl.-R.) calls "the first book of Enoch on the Egrēgoroi", but shows himself acquainted also with the subsequent chapters.[3]

It is noteworthy that Mani, who was brought up and spent most of his life in a province of the Persian empire, and whose mother belonged to a famous Parthian family,[4] did not make any use of the Iranian mythological tradition. There can no longer be any doubt that the Iranian names of Sām, Narīmān, etc., that appear in the Persian and Sogdian versions of the Book of the Giants, did not figure in the original edition, written by Mani in the Syriac language.[5] His disciples, who, it is well known, were in the habit of translating every word of a text (including the names of months, deities, etc.), seen fit also to "translate" the names of the giants. Thus Sām is merely the translation of Ohya. However, they kept some of the original names (e.g. Šhmyz'd), and adapted some others (e.g. Wrwgd'd).[6]

The story of the fallen angels and their giant sons needed little adaptation to be fitted into Mani's system. Of course, the heavenly origin of the B'nē-hā-Elōhīm[7] of Genesis vi, 2, 4, the Ἐγρήγοροι, of the Book of Enoch, did not square with Mani's conviction that no evil could come from good. Therefore he transformed them into "demons", namely those demons that when the world was being constructed had been imprisoned in the skies under the supervision of the Rex Honoris. They rebelled and were recaptured, but two hundred of them escaped to the earth. Mani also used the term Ἐγρήγοροι (preserved in Coptic, see texts L, M, P, S), or rather 'yr in Aramaic (once in a Middle Persian fragment, text D), but in Eastern sources they are mostly referred to as "demons" (Pers. dyw'n, Parth. dyw'n in T 6, Sogd. δywt in G, H 17, K 7, cytyt in E, δywt ZY ykšyšt in H. 16).

The puzzling clause of Genesis vi, 4: "The Nephilim were on the earth those days," was interpreted by Mani in this fashion: "when the Egrēgoroi descended, the animals, or proto-animals, were already in existence." Mani confused nəfīlīm with nefäl (näfäl) = ἔκτρωμα: see Nöldeke, ZDMG., 43 (1889), 536, who rightly referred to the formula of abjuration (P.Gr., i, 1461) where the giants and the "abortions" are mentioned in one breath. In Manichæan parlance, "abortion" (cf. also MPers. 'bg'ng, Sogd. pš'q) is synonymous with "animal".

We are therefore left with the Gibbōrīm, understood by Mani[8] as "giants". He probably used the equivalent Syriac word, gabbārē (gnbr'), which his disciples translated as γίγαντες, al-Jabābirah in Arabic, MPers. and Parthian k'w'n, Sogd. kwyšt = kawišt (Sing. qwy, kw'y = kawi); cf. Sb.P.A.W., 1934, 30. In Sasanian times the words derived from the Avestan Kavi were generally understood as "giant"; see Benveniste, MO., xxvi, 214, and Polotsky in Mir.Man., iii, 901. Thus MPers. Parth. k'w is freely used in Manichæan texts, e.g. of the Father of Light (M 40), of solar deities, of leading Manichæans (both in Mir.Man., iii), also of the First Man and Ahriman[9] with reference to the First Battle (which therefore could have been described as a γιγαντομαχία).[10] However, the word k'w is applied only to men and such beings as are imagined anthropomorphous. Where one would translate γίγας as monster, the Iranian equivalent is mzn, Mazan. Thus the γίγας τῆς θαλάσσης (Kephalaia, 113 and notes), whose breathing operations are responsible for ebb and flow (cf. also Beruni, India, 203, 10-11), is called Mzn 'y (z)rhyg[11] in Middle Persian (M 99, V 22-3). Accordingly, MPers. mzn (adj.[12] and noun) and the related words, Pahl. măzan, māzanīg, Sogd. mzny'n δyw, Av. māzainya-,[13] should be rendered as "monster", or "gigantic, monstrous".

The Egrēgoroi and their giant progeny are fought and vanquished by four archangels: Raphael, Michael, Gabriel, and Istrael (Enoch, 10, 1; or: Uriel, or: Fanuel). In the Book of the Giants they are called "the four angels". They are frequently invoked by name in Manichæan prayers (e.g. M 4 d 19, f 6; M 20), as Rwp'yl, Myx'yl, Gbr'yl, and Sr'yl (= Istrael).

There were no details about individual feats of the giants in the Book of Enoch. Mani filled the gap with the help of the above-mentioned Liber de Ogia nomine gigante. This Ogias has been identified with Og of Bashan,[14] who according to late sources lived five thousand years and managed to survive the Deluge, thanks to his giant size.[15] But possibly stories that primarily appertained to Ogias were transferred to the better known Og, owing to the resemblance of their names. The name of Ogias is 'why' ('why') = Ohyă (Oḥyă) in the Manichæan fragments, and this spelling is presumably more correct than that of Ogias. Og ('wg) indubitably would appear as 'wg (or: 'wg). Since Mani took 'why' from an Aramaic text, the ending of Ogias cannot be regarded as a Greek addition.

Ogias fought with a draco, and so did Ohya; his enemy was the Leviathan (text N). Ohya and his brother Ahya were the sons of Šhmyz'd (text H), i.e. Στμιαζᾶς, the chief of the Egrēgoroi in the Book of Enoch; hence, Στμιαζᾶς is transcription of šhm- (or šḥm ?). In the Persian edition of the Kawān Ohya and Ahya are "translated" as Sām and Narīmān, but the original names are kept in one passage (A 60). The translator did well to choose Sām-Krsāsp, both with regard to Ogias' longevity (Sām is one of the "Immortals") and to his fight with the dragon (Sām is a famous dragon-killer). In the Sogdian fragments the name of Sām is spelt S'hm = Sāhm, as it is often in Pahlavi (S'hm[16] beside S'm); Ṭabari has Shm,[17] cf. Christensen, Kayanides, p. 130. Sāhm's brother is Pāt-Sāhm. This name may have been invented by the Sogdian translator in order to keep the names of the brothers resembling each other. Narīmān was evidently not known in Sogdiana as a brother of Sām. According to the Book of the Giants, the main preoccupation of Sām-Sāhm was his quarrel the giant Māhawai,[18] the son of Virōgdād, who was one of the twenty ers of the Egrēgoroi.

The Book of the Giants was published in not less than six or seven languages. From the original Syriac the Greek and Middle Persian versions were made. The Sogdian edition was probably derived from the Middle Persian, the Uygur from the Sogdian.

There is no trace of a Parthian text.[19] The book may have existed in Coptic. The presence of names such as Sām and Narīmān in the Arabic version proves that it had been translated from the Middle Persian. To the few surviving fragments (texts A-G) I have added two excerpts, the more important of which (H) probably derives from a Syriac epitome of the book. Naturally, Manichæan authors quoted the book frequently, but there is only one direct citation by a non-Manichæan writer (text O). With the exception of text O, all the passages referring to the Book of the Giants (texts J-T) go back to Syriac writings (apparently). They are, therefore, to be treated as quotations from the Syriac edition. E.g. the Parthian text N is not the product of a Parthian writer who might have employed a Parthian version of the book, but was translated from a Syriac treatise whose author cited the Syriac text.

In their journey across Central Asia the stories of the Book of the Giants were influenced by local traditions. Thus, the translation of Ohya as Sām had in its train the introduction of myths appertaining to that Iranian hero; this explains the "immortality" of Sā(h)m according to text I. The country of Aryān-Vēžan = Airyana Vaēǰah, in text G (26), is a similar innovation.[20] The "Kögmän mountains" in text B may reflect the "Mount Hermon". The progeny of the fallen angels was confined in thirty-six towns (text S). Owing to the introduction of the Mount Sumeru, this number was changed (in Sogdiana) to thirty-two (text G, 22): "the heaven of Indra . . . is situated between the four peaks (cf. G 21) of the Meru, and consists of thirty-two cities of devas" (Eitel, Handb. Chinese Buddhism, 148, on Trayastriṃśat).

TEXTS

(bcd) = damaged letters, or uncertain readings.

[bcd] = suggested restorations of missing letters.

. . . = visible, but illegible letters.

[. . .] = estimated number of missing letters.

[   ] = a lacuna of undetermined extent.

(84)] = same, at the beginning of a line.

[(85 = same, at the end of a line.[21]

In the translation parentheses are employed for explanatory remarks.

FRAGMENTS OF THE KAWĀN

A. Middle-Persian

M 101, a to n, and M 911, fifteen fragments of a book, throughout small pieces from the centre of the pages. It has proved impossible, so far, to re-establish the original order of the pages. On purely technical grounds (size of the fragments, appearance of the margins, relative position of tears, stains, etc.), I at first assumed the following sequence: l-j-k-g-i-c-e-b-h-f-a-d-m-M 911-n. Being unable to estimate the cogency of these technical reasons now, because of the absence of any photographic material, I have decided to change the order of the first six fragments in the following way: c-j-l-k-g-i, in view of their contents.[22] Unfortunately we do not know in what order Mani had told the story of the giants. The task of finding the original order is made still more difficult by the fact that besides the Kawān the book contained one or two more treatises, namely: (1) Parables referring to the Hearers, and possibly (2) a discourse on the Five Elements (here (1) = lines 160 to the end, and (2) = lines 112-159). The only fragments that undoubtedly belonged to the Kawān are c-j-l-k-g-i, while the position of the fragments e-b-h is particularly doubtful. It must be borne in mind that whole folios may be missing between apparently successive pages. In order to enable the reader to judge for himself, all the fragments (including the parables) are published here. The text is based on a copy I made nearly ten years ago (referred to in the notes as: Copy); a revision is not possible under the present circumstances.

TRANSLATION

(Frg. c) . . . hard . . . arrow . . . bow, he that . . . Sām said: "Blessed be . . . had [he ?] seen this, he would not have died." Then Shahmīzād said to Sām, his [son]: "All that Māhawai . . ., is spoilt (?)." Thereupon he said to . . . "We are . . . until (10) . . and . . . (13) . . . that are in (?) the fiery hell (?) . . . As my father, Virōgdād, was . . ." Shahmīzād said: "It is true what he says. He says one of thousands.[23] For one of thousands . . . .". Sām thereupon began . . . Māhawai, too, in many places . . . (20) until to that place he might escape (1) and . . .[24]

(Frg. j) . . . Virōgdād . . . Hōbābīš [25] robbed Ahr . . . [26] of -naxtag,[27] his wife. Thereupon the giants began to kill each other and [to abduct their wives]. The creatures, too, began to kill each other.[28] Sām . . . before the sun, one hand in the air, the other (30) . . . whatever he obtained, to his brother . . . . imprisoned . . . (34) . . . over Taxtag.[29] To the angels . . . from heaven. Taxtag to . . . Taxtag threw (or: was thrown) into the water. Finally (?) . . . in his sleep Taxtag saw three signs, [one portending . . .], one woe and flight, and one . . . annihilation. Narīmān saw a gar[den full of] (40) trees in rows. Two hundred . . . came out, the trees. . . .[30]

(Frg. l) . . . Enoch,[31] the apostle, . . . [gave] a message to [the demons and their] children: To you . . . not peace.[32] [The judgment on you is] that you shall be bound for the sins you have committed.[33] You shall see the destruction of your children.[34] ruling for a hundred and twenty[35] [years] . . . . (50) . . . wild ass, ibex . . . ram, goat (?),[36] gazelle, . . . oryx, of each two hundred, a pair[37] . . . the other wild beasts, birds, and animals and their wine [shall be] six thousand jugs . . . irritation(?)[38] of water (?) . . . and their oil shall be [39] . . .

(Frg. k) . . . father . . . nuptials (?) . . . until the completion of his . . . in fighting . . . (60) . . . and in the nest(?) Ohya and Ahya . . . he said to his brother: "get up and . . . we will take what our father has ordered us to. The pledge we have given . . . battle." And the giants . . . together . . . (67) "[Not the] . . . of the lion, but the . . . on his . . . [Not the] . . . of the rainbow, but the bow . . . firm. Not the sharpness of the blade, [but] (70) the strength of the ox (?).[40] Not the . . . eagle, but his wings.[41] Not the . . . gold, but the brass that hammers[42] it. Not the proud [ruler], but the diadem on his [head. Not] the splendid cypress, but the . . . of the mountain . . .

(Frg. g) . . . Not he that engages in quarrels, but he that is true in his speech. Not the evil fruit(?), but the poison in it. (80) [Not they that] are placed (?) [43] in the skies but the God [of all] worlds. Not the servant is proud, but [the lord] that is above him. Not one that is sent . . ., but the man that sent him".[44] Thereupon Narīmān . . . said . . . (86) . . . And (in) another place I saw those that were weeping for the ruin that had befallen them, and whose cries and laments rose up to heaven. (90) And also I saw another place [where there were] tyrants and rulers . . . in great number, who had lived [45] in sin and evil deeds, when [46] . . .

(Frg. i) [47] . . . many . . . were killed, four hundred thousand Righteous [48] . . . with fire, naphtha, and brimstone [49] . . . And the angels veiled [50] (or: covered, or: protected, or: moved out of sight) Enoch. Electae et auditrices (100) . . . and ravished them. They chose beautiful [women], and demanded . . . them in marriage.[51] Sordid . . . (103) . . . all . . . carried off . . . severally they were subjected to tasks and services. And they . . . from

each city . . . and were, ordered to serve the . . . The Mesenians
[were directed] to prepare, the Khūzians [52] to sweep [and] (110)
water, the Persians to . . .

[On the Five Elements]

(Frg. e) (112) . . . slaying . . . righteous . . . good deeds . . . .
elements. The crown, the diadem, [the garland, and] the
garment (of Light). The seven demons. Like a blacksmith [who]
binds (or: shuts, fastens) and looses (or: opens, detaches) . . . .
who from the seeds of . . . . and serves the king . . . . (120) . . .
offends . . . when weeping . . . with mercy . . . hand . . . (125) p.
63 . . . the Pious gave . . . ? . . . presents. Some buried the idols.
The Jews did good and evil. Some make their god half demon,
half god . . . (130) killing . . . the seven demons . . . eye . . .

(Frg. b) . . . various colours that by . . . and bile. If. . . . from the
five elements. As if (it were) a means not to die, they fill
themselves with food and drink. Their (140) garment is . . . this
corpse . . . and not firm . . . Its ground is not firm . . . Like . . .
(146) . . . imprisoned [in this corpse], in bones, nerves,[53] [flesh],
veins, and skin, and entered herself [= Āz] into it. Then he (=
Man) cries out, over [54] (?) sun and moon, the Just God's (150)
two flames [55] . . . ? . . .,[56] over the elements, the trees and the
animals. But God [Zrwān ?], in each epoch,[57] sends apostles:
Šīt[īl, Zarathushtra,] Buddha, Christ, . . .

(Frg. h) . . . evil-intentioned . . . from where . . . he came. The
Misguided recognize the five elements, [the five kinds of] trees,
the five (kinds of) animals.

(160) . . . On the Hearers

. . . we receive . . . from Mani, the Lord, . . . the Five Com-
mandments to . . . the Three Seals . . . (164) . . . living . . .

profession . . . and wisdom . . . moon. Rest from the power (or: deceit) . . . own. And keep measured the mixture (?) . . . trees and wells, in two . . . (170) water, and fruit, milk, . . . he should not offend his brother. The wise [Hearer] who like unto juniper [leaves [58] . .

(Frg. f) . . . much profit. Like a farmer . . . who sows seed . . in many [59] . . . The Hearer who . . . knowledge, is like unto a man that threw (the dish called) [60] frōšag (180) [into] milk(?). It became hard, not . . . The part that ruin . . . at first heavy. Like . . . first . . . is honoured . . . might shine . . . (188) six days. The Hearer who gives alms (to the Elect), is like unto a poor (190) man that presents his daughter to the king; he reaches (a position of) great honour.[61] In the body of the Elect the (food given to to him as) alms is purified in the same manner as a . . . that by fire and wind . . . beautiful clothes on a clean body . . . turn . . .

(Frg. a) . . . witness . . . fruit . . . (200) . . . tree . . . like firewood . . . like a grain (?) . . . radiance. The Hearer in [the world ?], (and) the alms within the Church, are like unto a ship [on the sea] [62]: the towing-line [63] (is) in the hand of [the tower] on shore, the sailor (210) is [on board the ship]. The sea is the world, the ship is [the . . ., the . . . is the ?al]ms, the tower is [the . . . ?], the towing-line (?) is the Wisdom. . . . . . . (214) . . . The Hearer . . . is like unto the branch (?) of a fruitless [tree] . . . fruitless . . . and the Hearers . . . fruit that . . . (220) pious deeds. [The Elect,] the Hearer, and Vahman, are like unto three brothers to whom some [possessions] were left by their father: a piece of land, . . ., seed. They became partners . . . they reap and . . . The Hearer . . . like . . .

(Frg. d) . . . an image (?) of the king, cast of gold . . . (230) . . . the king gave presents. The Hearer that copies a book, is like unto a sick man that gave his . . . [64] to a . . . man. The Hearer that gives [his] daughter to the church,[65] is like . . . pledge, who (= father ?) gave his son to . . . learn . . . to . . . father, pledge . . . (240) . . . Hearer. Again, the Hearer . . . is like . . . . stumble . . . is purified. To . . . the soul from the Church, is like unto the wife of the soldier (or: Roman) who . . . infantrist, one shoe . . . who, however, with a denarius . . . was. The wind tore out one . . . he was abashed [66] . . . from the ground . . . ground . . .

(Frg. m) . . . (250) . . . sent . . . The Hearer that makes one . . ., is like unto [a compassionate mother] who had seven sons . . . the enemy [killed] all . . . The Hearer that . . . piety . . . (258) . . . a well. One [on the shore of] the sea, one in the boat. (260) [He that is on] shore, tows(?) him that is [in the boat].[67] He that is in the boat. . . . sea. Upwards to . . . like . . ? . . like a pearl . . . diadem . . .

(Frg. M 911) . . . Church. Like unto a man that . . . fruit and flowers . . . then they praise . . . fruitful tree . . . (270) . . . [Like unto a man] that bought a piece of land. [On that] piece of land [there was] a well, [and in that well a bag] full of drachmas . . . the king was filled with wonder . . . share . . . pledge . . .

(Frg. n) . . . numerous . . . Hearer. At . . . like unto a garment . . . (280) like . . . to the master . . . like . . . and a blacksmith. The goldsmith . . . to honour, the blacksmith to . . . one to . . .

B. Uygur

LeCoq, Türk. Man., iii, 23. Bang, Muséon, xliv, 13-17. Order of pages according to LeCoq (the phot. publ. by Bang seems to support LeCoq's opinion).

(First page) . . . fire was going to come out. And [I saw] that the sun was at the point of rising, and that [his ?] centre (orḍu) without increasing (? ašïlmatïn ?) above was going to start rolling. Then came a voice from the air above. Calling me, it spoke thus: "Oh son of Virōgdād, your affairs are lamentable (?). More than this you shall [not] see. Do not die now prematurely, but turn quickly back from here." And again, besides this (voice), I heard the voice of Enoch, the apostle, from the south, without, however, seeing him at all. Speaking my name very lovingly, he called. And downwards from . . . then

(Second page) . . . " . . for the closed [68] door of the sun will open, the sun's light and heat will descend and set your wings alight. You will burn and die," said he. Having heard these words, I beat my wings and quickly flew down from the air. I looked back: Dawn had . . . ., with the light of the sun it had come to rise over the Kögmän mountains. And again a voice came from above. Bringing the command of Enoch, the apostle, it said: "I call you, Virōgdād, . . . I know . . . his direction . . . you . . . you . . . Now quickly . . . people . . . also . . .

C. Sogdian

M 648. Small scrap from the centre of a page. Order of pages uncertain.

(First page) . . . I shall see. Thereupon now S[āhm, the giant] was [very] angry, and laid hands on M[āhawai, the giant], with the intention: I shall . . . and kill [you]. Then . . . the other g[iants . . .

(Second page) . . . do not be afraid, for . . . [Sā]hm, the giant, will want to [kill] you, but I shall not let him . . . I myself shall damage . . . Thereupon Māhawai, the g[iant], . . . was satisfied . . .

D. Middle-Persian

Published Sb.P.A.W., 1934, p. 29.

. . . outside . . . and . . . left . . . . read the dream we have seen. Thereupon Enoch thus . . . . and the trees that came out, those are the Egrēgoroi ('yr), and the giants that came out of the women. And . . . . . over . . . pulled out . . . over . . .

E. Sogdian

T iii 282. Order of pages uncertain.

(First page) . . . [when] they saw the apostle, . . . before the apostle . . . those demons that were [timid], were very, very glad at seeing the apostle. All of them assembled before him. Also, of those that were tyrants and criminals, they were [worried] and much afraid.[69] Then . . .

(Second page) . . . not to . . . Thereupon those powerful demons spoke thus to the pious apostle [70]: If . . . . by us any (further) sin [will] not [be committed ?], my lord, why ? . . . . you have . . . and weighty injunction [71] . . .

F. Middle-Persian

T ii D ii 164. Six fragmentary columns, from the middle of a page. Order of columns uncertain. Instead of A///B///CDEF, it might have been: BCDEFA, or even CDEF///A///B.[72]

(Col. A) . . . poverty . . . [those who] harassed [73] the happiness of the Righteous, on that account they shall fall into eternal ruin and distress, into that Fire, the mother of all conflagrations and the foundation of all ruined tyrants. And when these sinful misbegotten sons [74] of ruin in those crevices and . . . .

(Col. B) . . . you have not been better. In error you thought you would this false power eternally.[75] You . . . all this iniquity . . .

(Col. C) . . . you that call to us with the voice of falsehood. Neither did we reveal ourselves on your account, so that you could see us, nor thus . . . . ourselves through the praise and greatness that to us . . . -given to you . . ., but . . .

(Col. D) . . . sinners . . . . . is visible, where out of this fire your soul will be prepared (for the transfer) to eternal ruin (?). And as for you, sinful misbegotten sons of the Wrathful Self,[76] confounders of the true words of that Holy One, disturbers of the actions of Good Deed, aggressors upon Piety, . . . -ers of the Living. . . ., who their . . .

(Col. E) . . . and on brilliant wings they shall fly and soar further outside and above that Fire, and shall gaze into its depth and height. And those Righteous that will stand around it, outside and above, they themselves shall have power over that Great Fire, and over everything in it. . . . . . blaze . . . . souls that . . .

(Col. F) . . . they are purer and stronger [than the] Great Fire of Ruin that sets the worlds ablaze. They shall stand around it, outside and above, and splendour shall shine over them. Further outside and above it they shall fly [77] (?) after those souls that may try to escape from the Fire. And that . . . .

G. Sogdian

T ii. Two folios (one only publ. here; the other contains a wyδβ'γ cn pš'q̱t δγwtyy "Discourse on the Nephīlīm-demons"). Headlines: R: pš'n prβ'r [78] ". . . pronouncement", V: iv fryštyt δn CC "The four angels with the two hundred [demons . . . ".

. . . they took and imprisoned all the helpers that were in the heavens. And the angels themselves descended from the heaven to the earth. And (when) the two hundred demons saw those angels, they were much afraid and worried. They assumed the shape of men [79] and hid themselves. Thereupon the angels forcibly removed the men [80] from the demons, (10) laid them aside, and put watchers over them . . . . the giants . . . . were sons . . . with each other in bodily union . . . . with each other self- . . . . and the . . . . that had been born to them, they forcibly removed them [81] from the demons. And they led one half of them (20) eastwards, and the other half westwards, on the skirts of four huge mountains, towards the foot of the Sumeru mountain, into thirty-two towns which the Living Spirit had prepared for them in the beginning.[82] And one calls (that place) Aryān-waižan. And those men are (or: were) . . . . in the first arts and crafts.[83] (30) . . . . they made . . . the angels . . . and to the demons . . . they went to fight. And those two hundred demons fought a hard battle with the [four angels], until [the angels used] fire, naphtha, and brimstone [84] . . . .

EXCERPTS

H. Sogdian

T ii S 20. Sogdian script.[85] Two folios. Contents similar to the "Kephalaia". Only about a quarter (I R i-17) publ. here. The following chapter has as headline: ''γšt š'nš'y cnn 'β[c'n]pδ[yh w]prs = Here begins: Šanšai's [86] question the world. Init. rty tym ZK š'nš'[y] [cnn] m'rm'ny rwyšny pr'yš[t'kw w'nkw ']prs' 'yn'k 'βc'npδ ZY kw ZKh mrtymyt ('skw'nt) oo ckn'c pyδ'r ''zy mrch 'zγyr'nt = And again Šanšai asked the Light Apostle: this world where mankind lives, why does one call it birth-death (saṃsāra, Chin. shêng-szŭ).

... and what they had seen in the heavens among the gods, and also what they had seen in hell, their native land, and furthermore what they had seen on earth,—all that they began to teach (hendiadys) to the men.[87] To Šahmīzād two(?) sons were borne by .... One of them he named "Ohya"; in Sogdian he is called "Sāhm, the giant". And again a second son [was born] to him. He named him "Ahya"; its Sogdian (equivalent) is "Pāt-Sāhm". As for the remaining giants, they were born to the other demons and Yakṣas. (Colophon) Completed: (the chapter on) "The Coming of the two hundred Demons".

I. Sogdian

M 500 n. Small fragment.

.... manliness, in powerful tyranny, he (or: you ?) shall not die". The giant Sāhm and his brother will live eternally. For in the whole world in power and strength, and in .... [they have no equal].

QUOTATIONS AND ALLUSIONS

J. Middle-Persian

T ii D ii 120, V ii 1-5: and in the coming of the two hundred demons there are two paths: the hurting speech, and the hard labour; these (belong, or: lead) to hell.

K. Sogdian

M 363.

(First page) ... before ... they were. And all the ... [88] fulfilled their tasks lawfully. Now, they became excited and irritated for the following reason: namely, the two hundred demons came down to the sphere from the high heaven, and the . . . .

(Second page) . . . in the world they became excited and irritated. For their life-lines and the connections of their Pneumatic Veins [89] are joined to sphere. (Colophon) Completed: the exposition of the three worlds. (Head-line) Here begins: the coming of Jesus and [his bringing] the religion to Adam and Šitil. . . . you should care and . . .

L. Coptic

Kephalaia, 17116-19: Earthquake and malice happened in the watchpost of the Great King of Honour, namely the Egrēgoroi who arose at the time when they were . . . . and there descended those who were sent to confound them.

M. Coptic

Kephalaia, 9224-31: Now attend and behold how the Great King of Honour who is ἔννοια, is in the third heaven. He is . . . with the wrath . . . and a rebellion . . ., when malice and wrath arose in his camp, namely the Egrēgoroi of Heaven who in his watch-district (rebelled and) descended to the earth. They did all deeds of malice. They revealed the arts in the world, and the mysteries of heaven to the men. Rebellion and ruin came about on the earth . . .

N. Parthian

M 35, lines 21-36. Fragment of a treatise entitled 'rdhng wyfr's = Commentary on (Mani's opus) Ārdahang.[90]

And the story about the Great Fire: like unto (the way in which) the Fire, with powerful wrath, swallows this world and enjoys it;

like unto (the way in which) this fire that is in the body, swallows the exterior fire that is (lit. comes) in fruit and food, and enjoys it. Again, like unto (the story in which) two brothers who found a treasure, and a pursuer lacerated each other, and they died; like unto (the fight in which) Ohya, Lewyātīn (= Leviathan), and Raphael lacerated each other, and they vanished; like unto (the story in which) a lion cub, a calf in a wood (or: on a meadow), and a fox lacerated each other, [and they vanished, or: died]. Thus [the Great Fire swallows, etc.] both of the fires. . . .[91]

M 740. Another copy of this text.

O. Arabic, from Middle-Persian ? [92]

Al-Ghaḍanfar (Abū Isḥāq Ibr. b. Muḥ. al-Tibrīzī, middle of thirteenth century), in Sachau's edition of Beruni's Āthār al-bāqiyah, Intr., p. xiv: The Book of the Giants, by Mani of Babylon, is filled with stories about these (antediluvian) giants, amongst whom Sām and Narīmān.

P. Coptic

Keph. 9323-28: On account of the malice and rebellion that had arisen in the watch-post of the Great King of Honour, namely the Egrēgoroi who from the heavens had descended to the earth,—on their account the four angels received their orders: they bound the Egrēgoroi with eternal fetters in the prison of the Dark(?), their sons were destroyed upon the earth.

Q. Coptic

Manich. Psalm-book, ed. Allberry, 1427-9: The Righteous who were burnt in the fire, they endured. This multitude that were wiped out, four thousand . . . . Enoch also, the Sage, the transgressors being . . .

R. Coptic

Man. Homil., ed. Polotsky, 6818-19: . . . evil. 400,000 Righteous . . . . the years of Enoch . . .

S. Coptic

Keph., 1171-9: Before the Egrēgoroi rebelled and descended from heaven, a prison had been built for them in the depth of the earth beneath the mountains. Before the sons of the giants were born who knew not Righteousness and Piety among themselves, thirty-six towns had been prepared and erected, so that the sons of the giants should live in them, they that come to beget . . . . who live a thousand years.

T. Parthian

291a. Order of pages unknown.

(First page) . . . mirror . . . image. . . . distributed. The men . . . and Enoch was veiled (= moved out of sight).[93] They took . . . Afterwards, with donkey-goads . . . . slaves,[94] and waterless trees (?). Then . . . and imprisoned the demons. And of them . . . . seven and twelve.

(Second page) . . . three thousand two hundred and eighty-[95] . . . the beginning of King Vištāsp.[96] . . . . in the palace he flamed forth (or: in the brilliant palace). And at night . . ., then to the broken gate . . . men . . . physicians, merchants, farmers, . . . at sea. ? . . . armoured he came out . .

APPENDIX

U. Parthian

T ii D 58. From the end (. . . r š t) of a hymn.

. . . gifts. A peaceful sovereign [was] King Vištāsp, [in Aryā]n-
Waižan [97]; Wahman and Zarēl . . . . The sovereign's queen,
Khudōs,[98] received the Faith,[99] the prince . . . They have secured
(a place in) the (heavenly) hall, and quietude for ever and ever .
. .

V. Sogdian

M 692. Small fragment. Order of pages uncertain.

(First page) . . . because . . . the House of the Gods, eternal joy,
and good . . ? . .[100] For so it is said: at that time . . . Yima was . . .
in the world. And at the time of the new moon (?) . . . . the
blessed denizens of the world [101] . . . all assembled [102] . . . all . . .

(Second page) . . . they offered five garlands in homage.[103] And
Yima accepted those garlands . . . And those . . . that . . . . and
great kingship . . . was his. And on . . . them . . . . And acclama-
tions [104] . . . And from that pious (?) . . . he placed the garlands
on his head . . . the denizens of the world . . .

ENDNOTES

[1] Numerous variants (p. 126, Dobschütz), e.g. de ogiae, de oggie, diogiae, diogine, diogenes, de ozia, de ugia, de ugica, de ogiga, de eugia, de uegia, de eugenia, etc. In Migne's Patrologia Latina the text is in vol. 59, 162-3. (p. 1)

[2] See Charles, The Book of Enoch, 2nd ed., 1912. For the Greek fragments (and Georgius S.) the edition by Flemming and Radermacher (= Fl.-R.) is quoted here. For Mani's use of the Enoch literature see my papers in Sb.P.A.W., 1934, 27-32, and in ZDMG., 90, 2-4. (p. 1)

[3] See below A 86-94, and compare G 19-21 with Enoch 67, 4, and G 38 with Enoch 17, 1; 21, 7; 54, 6; 67, 4-13. On chaps. 72 sqq. see Sb.P.A.W., 1934, 32. (p. 1)

[4] Namely the Kamsarakan-k' (mentioned often in the Armenian history of the fourth century) who claimed descent from the royal house of the Arsacids. This is clear from the Chinese-Manichæan text that preceded the Fragment Pelliot, now printed in the Taishô Tripiṭaka as No. 2141a, vol. 54, p. 1280A, but hitherto untranslated: "He was born in the country of Sulin (= Babylonia), in the royal abode of B'uât-tiei (= Patī-g), by his wife Muân-ẗäm (= Maryam) of the family of Ḳẖəm-sât-g'iɒn (= Kamsar(a)gān)." The name Κάρασσα in the Byzantine formula of abjuration (Migne, Patr. Gr., i, 1468) may be corrupted from Kamsar-. Thus there is a grain of truth in the assertion in the K. al-Fihrist, 327, 31, that Mani's mother had belonged to the Arsacid house; ibid., Maryam (ed, marmaryam) is given as one of her names.— It is not proposed to discuss the origin of Mani's father here. (p. 1)

[5] I have abandoned my earlier opinion on this point (ZDMG., 90, 4) which was based on insufficient material. The important Sogdian fragment, text H, was not then known to me. (p. 2)

[6] See BSOS., viii, 583; ZDMG., 90, 4. [Cf. also Bal. girōk, Geiger, No.107.] (p. 2)

[7] of the B'nē-hā-Elōhīm2 (p. 2)

[8] Herein he differed from the common interpretation of the passage (Nephilim = giants), shared also by the authors of the Book of Enoch. (p. 3)

[9] M 41: 'br q'rc'r 'wt̲ zmbg 'stft cy 'whrmyzdbg qyrd 'd dyw'n: dw q'w'n 'wt̲ dw nyw'n. (p. 3)

[10] This word, in the anti-Manichæan book by Alexander Lycopolitanus, p. 8, 10, ed. Brinkmann, refers neither to the Manich. "First Battle", nor to Mani's Book of the Giants, as Cumont, Rech., i, 3; ii, 160 sq., erroneously states. Cumont goes so far as to say that in the quoted passage Alexander had given a summary of Mani's work, and Benveniste, MO., xxvi, 213, has repeated this statement. In fact, Alexander says that experts in Greek mythology might quote, from p. 54 the Greek poets, the Greek γιγαντομαχία, as a parallel to the Manich. doctrine of the rising by the Hyle against God. In ch. 25 (p. 37, 13 sqq.) Alexander explains that such poetical fables about giants could not be regarded as a satisfactory parallel, because they were myths and meant to be understood as allegories. He then (37, 17) quotes the story of Genesis vi, 2-4, which he provides with an allegorical explanation. But he ascribes it to the History of the Jews without even mentioning the Book of the Giants. This shows conclusively that he had no knowledge of Mani's book. (p. 3)

[11] Jackson, Researches, 37, 67 sq., has "poisonous mass"; cf. OLZ., 1934, 752. (p. 3)

[12] Hence the comparative mzndr (e.g. Mir.Man., i) and the superlative Pahl. măzan-tum (e.g. Dd., p. 118, 12 ed. Anklesaria). (p. 3)

[13] Clearly to be derived from Av. mazan- "greatness". Cf. also Jackson, loc. cit., on mzn. Hence, the first part of the name of Māzandarān probably = "gigantic". (p. 3)

[14] Thus Dobschütz, Decret. Gelas., p. 305. (p. 3)

[15] Dobschütz, loc. cit., who quotes Fabricius, Cod. pseudepigr., 799 sq., and Migne, Dict. des apocr., ii, 649, 1295. (p. 4)

[16] For example, Men.Khr., 68, 12; 69, 12, ed. Andreas; Pahl. Yasna, 9, 10 (p. 71, 19). (p. 4)

[17] Shm, of course, transcribes S'hm, not S'm. (p. 4)

[18] MPers. m'hw'y A 7, with suff. m'hwy-c A 19, Sogd. m'h'wy C 15 (= Wrogdad oylï in B). Hardly = Māhōi (as suggested ZDMG., 90, 4), for the ending -ōi was pronounced -ōi also in the third century (cf. e.g. wyrwd = Wērōi in the inscription of Shapur, line 34). Furthermore, there was no Māhōi among the heroes of the Iranian epos (M. is well known as the name of the governor of Marv at the time of the last Yezdegerd). More likely Māhawai was a non-Iranian name and figured already in the Aramaic edition of the Kawān; it may have been adapted to Persian. Cf. Mḥwy'l, Genesis, iv, 18 ? (p. 4)

[19] But see Mir.Man., iii, 858 (b 134 sqq.). (p. 5)

[20] The children of the Egrēgoroi share with the inhabitants of Airyana Vaēĵah the distinction of being regarded as the inventors (or first users) of the arts and crafts. For the spelling of Aryān-Vēžan see also Appendix, text U. It is not clear whether Yima (text V) had been given a place in the Sogdian Kawān. Ymyḫ, i.e. Imi, is the correct Sogdian form of the name. (p. 5)

[21] This system of notation has been used also in my book Sogdica, and in my paper in BSOS., X, pp. 941 sqq. The various interpunction marks are uniformly represented by oo here. (p. 6)

[22] But possibly Frg. i should occupy the first place; see below, notes on lines 95-111. (p. 6)

[23] = far less than he could say. Cf. əž hazār yak, ŠGV., xiv, 2, əž hazārą baewarą yak, ibid., xvi, 1. Salemann, Zap. Imp. Ak. Nauk, sér. viii, t. vi, No. 6, 25, quoted Persian az hazār yakī va az bisyār andakī. (p. 8)

[24] The texts B and C (Uygur and Sogdian) could be inserted here (or hereabouts). (p. 8)

[25] Probably one of the twenty "decarchs" (Enoch 6, 7), viz. No. 4 Kokabiel = Χωχαριήλ in the Greek fragments, and Χωβαβιήλ apud Syncellus. (p. 8)

[26] This also could be a "decarch", Arakib- Ἀρακιήλ, or Aramiel-Ῥαμιήλ. (p. 8)

[27] Incomplete name. (p. 8)

[28] Cf. Enoch 7, 5. (p. 8)

[29] txtg might be appellative, = "a board". This would fit in three of the passages, but hardly in the fourth. (p. 8)

[30] Evidently this is the dream that Enoch reads in the fragment M 625c (= Text D, below), which therefore probably belonged to the Kawān. It should be inserted here. (p. 8)

[31] Here (or hereabouts) the texts E and F should be entered, both of which deal with the judgment on the fallen angels. Text F approximates to Enoch, ch. 10 (pronouncement of the judgment by God), while Text E is nearer to Enoch, ch. 13 (communication of the judgment the angels by Enoch). (p. 8)

[32] = Enoch, 12, 4-5: εἰπὲ τοῖς ἐγρηγόροις . . . . οὐκ ἔσται ὑμῖν εἰρήνη. (p. 8)

[33] = Enoch, 13, 1-2: ὁ δὲ 'Ενώχ . . . εἶπεν . . . οὐκ ἔσται σοι εἰρήνη κρῖμα μέγα ἐξῆλθεν κατὰ σοῦ δῆσαί σε . . . περί . . . τῆς ἀδικίας καὶ τῆς ἁμαρτίας κτλ. (p. 8)

[34] = Enoch, 14, 6: ἴδητε τὴν ἀπώλειαν τῶν υἱῶν ὑμῶν. (p. 8)

[35] = Syncellus, pp. 44-5 Fl.-R. (ad cap. xvi), cf. Genesis, vi, 3. ἀπολοῦνται οἱ ἀγαπητοὶ ὑμῶν . . . . ὅτι πᾶσαι αἱ ἡμέραι τῆς ζωῆς αὐτῶν ἀπὸ τοῦ νῦν οὐ μὴ ἔσονται πλείω τῶν ἑκατὸν εἴκοσιν ἐτῶν. (p. 8)

[36] In Jewish Persian trwš is "ram" (Lagarde, Pers. Stud., 73), but in the dialect of Rīšahr nr. Bushire (according to the notes made on this dialect by Andreas about seventy years ago) tîštär is "a young she-goat". See JRAS., 1942, 248. [trwš, Is. 111, ler. 5140 = Hebr. ʿattūd, probably understood as "he-goat".] (p. 8)

[37] These lines evidently refer to the promise of peace and plenty that concludes the divine judgment in Enoch, 10. Hence = "each pair of those animals shall have two hundred young"? (p. 8)

[38] sārišn: cf. DkM. 487apu.-488, 3, "when they provoke (sārēn-) him he does not get irritated (sār- and better, sārih-)." GrBd. 5, 8, "if you do not provoke, or instigate (sārēn-) a fight" (differently Nyberg, ii, 202). sār-, if from sarəd- (Skt. śardh-), is presumably the transitive to syrydn (from srdhya- according to Bartholomæ), cf. NGGW., 1932, 215, n. 3. (p. 9)

[39] Cf. Enoch, 10, 19: ἡ ἄμπελος [sic] ἣν ἂν φυτεύσωσιν ποιήσουσιν πρόχους οἴνου χιλιάδας . . . . ἐλαίας . . . . (p. 9)

[40] ty or ty[y] = tai from taih from taiɣ (cf. GGA., 1935, 18), is ambiguous: (1) sharp instrument, (2) burning, glow, brightness, sunrays, etc. So also is tyzyy: (1) sharpness, (2) speed. One could also restore ty[gr]. (p. 9)

[41] Lit. "but the Wing(s) that (is, are) with him." The curious expression was chosen probably on account of the rhythm. For the same reason byc is employed in the place of 'n'y in line 73. (p. 9)

[42] Lit. "beats". (p. 9)

[43] ystyh- is obviously different from 'styh- (on which see BSOS., IX, 81), and possibly derived from 'yst-, cf. z'yh- "to be born" from z'y- "to be born". 'ystyh- is met with in W.-L., ii, 558, p. 62 Ri 25, "blessed chief who stands ('ystyhyd ?) as the sign of the Light Gods." Lentz has 'ystyhnd, but without having seen the manuscript one may presume a misreading (cf. ibid., R i l, Lentz: pd[. .]dg, but probably pr['d]ng, R i 2, Lentz: p.d'r, but probably pyr'r, ibid., R ii 22, Lentz: 'n.z, but probably "wn; for further cases see OLZ., 1934, 10). (p. 9)

[44] St. John, 13, 18. (p. 9)

[45] phrystn: phryz- = Parth. prx'štn: prxyz- (cf. Av. pārihaēza-, Sogd. pr-yyž; Parth. 'x'št: MPers. 'xyst) is mostly "to stand around, to be about, versari", sometimes "to stand around for the purpose of looking after someone" = "serve, nurse, protect", often merely "to be". phryz- "to stand off, to abstain" is presumably different (para-haēza-). (p. 9)

[46] The series of visions in which Enoch sees the arrangements for the punishment of the fallen angels, etc., and of "the kings and the Mighty" (chaps. xvii sqq.), follows immediately upon the announce-ment of the divine judgment. Hence, frgg. k-g must be placed after frg. I. Text G (below), which describes, the execution of the divine order, could perhaps be inserted here. (p. 9)

[47] It is difficult to decide whether this fragment should be placed at the end or at the beginning of the book. The 400,000 Righteous may have perished when the Egrēgoroi descended to the earth. The "choosing of beautiful women", etc., strongly suggests the misbehaviour of the Egrēgoroi on their arrival upon the earth. The hard labour imposed on the Mesenians and other nations may be due to the insatiable needs of their giant progeny (Enoch, 7, 2 sqq.). On the other hand, "fire,

naphtha, and brimstone" are only mentioned as the weapons with which the archangels overcame the Egrēgoroi, after a prolonged and heavy fight (Text G, 38), and the 400,000 Righteous may well have been the innocent non-combatant victims of this battle which may have had a demoralizing effect even upon the electae. To clear up the debris the archangels would naturally commandeer the men. We do not know whether Mani believed Enoch to have been moved out of sight (ἐλήμφθη Enoch, 12, 1) before the Egrēgoroi appeared, or before they were punished. (p. 9)

[48] See texts R, and Q (where 4,000 instead of 400,000). (p. 9)

[49] See BSOS., X, 398. (p. 9)

[50] See text T, line 3. (p. 9)

[51] Cf. Enoch, 7, 1 ? (p. 9)

[52] On myšn'yg'n see BSOS., X, 945, n. 2, on hwjyg, ibid., 944, n. 7. (p. 10)

[53] py(y) always = nerves, sinews (not "fat" as in Mir.Man., i, etc., as alternative rendering). It is equivalent to nerfs (Chavannes-Pelliot, Traité Man., 32/3 [528/9]), Uygur singir (T.M., iii, 18/9), Copt. = Sehne (Keph., 96, etc.), Sogd. pδδw' (unpubl.). Cf. also GrBd., 196, 4, where Goetze, ZII., ii, 70, wrongly has "fat". MPers. pai = NPers. pai = Pashto pala = Sogd. pδδw' (not Av. piθwā-). (p. 10)

[54] Hardly "to". Cf. Cumont, Rech., i, 49, and my paper NGGW., 1932, 224. (p. 10)

[55] Or: over the Just God, sun and moon, the (or: his) two flames. The "Just God" is the Messenger (not = bgr'štygr, i.e. Zrwān). (p. 10)

[56] Unintelligible. Lit. ". . . two flames given into the (or: his) hand". (p. 10)

[57] Cf. Sb.P.A.W., 1934, 27, and BSOS., VIII, 585. (p. 10)

[58] Cf. M 171, 32 sqq. 'wt̲ 'st ngwš'g ky 'w 'b[w](r)[s] m'nh'g ky hmyw zrgwng 'štyd 'wš zmg 'wd t'b'n png ny ryzynd. 'w'gwn hwyc hwrw'n ngwš'g pd pzd 'wd wšyd'x pd xw'r 'wt̲ dyjw'r, kd dwr 'c wjydg'n 'wt̲ kd nzd 'w wjydg'n, hw pd wxybyy frhyft 'wd w'wryft 'škbyd, etc. "And some Hearers are like unto the juniper which is ever green, and whose leaves are shed neither in summer nor in winter. So also the pious Hearer, in times of persecution and of free exercise (lit. open-mindedness), in good and bad days, under the eyes of the Elect or out of their sight,—he is constant in his charity and faith." Although the word 'brws is incomplete in both passages, its restoration is practically a certainty. (p. 11)

[59] Possibly the parable of St. Mark, iv, 3 sqq. (p. 11)

[60] BSOS., IX, 86. (p. 11)

[61] An elaborate version of this parable is found in M 221 R 9-23: u nywš'g ky h'n rw'ng'n 'w wjyydg'n ''wryyd, ''wn m'n'g c'wn 'škwh̲ myrd [ky] dwxt 'y nyq z'd hy, 'wd pd wryhryy 'wd 'gr'yyh̲ 'byr hwcyyhr hy. 'wd h'n myrd 'y 'škwh̲ 'w hwcyhryyh̲ 'y 'wy qnyycg xwyš dwxtr prg' myyh̲ cy 'byr h[wcyhr] [h]y. 'wd 'wy dwxtr 'y hwcyhr [   ]. 'wš 'w š'h̲ hndyym'n [qwnyh̲] 'wd š'h̲ 'wy qnycg ps[ndyh̲ ?] 'wd pd znyy nš'yy. 'wš [   ] pws 'cyyš z'ynd[   ] pwsryn 'yš 'c 'w[y myrd 'y 'š]kwh̲ dwxtr z['d (remainder missing), "The Hearer that brings alms to the Elect, is like unto a poor man to whom a pretty daughter has been born, who is very beautiful with charm and loveliness. That poor man fosters the beauty of that girl, his daughter, for she is very beautiful. And that beautiful daughter, he presents her to the king. The king approves of her, and puts her into his harem. He has [several] sons by her. The sons that were born to that poor man's daughter . . . .". Throughout the story the parabolic optative is in use. (p. 11)

[62] For a similar parable see below, lines 258 sqq. (p. 11)

[63] zyyg: this word, hitherto unexplained, occurs in the Šābuhragān (M 470 V 14, spelt z'yg). The sinners, roasting in hell, see the Righteous enjoying the New Paradise, and ask them: . . . 'wm'n . . . z'yg 'w dst dyy[d 'wd ']c 'yn swcyšn bwzy[d] ". . . put a rope (or: life-line) in our hands and rescue us from this conflagration". Cf. Pahl., Pers. zīg, Nyberg, Mazd. Kal., 68. (p. 11)

[64] Possibly "weapons". (p. 12)

[65] Cf. Kephalaia, 192/3. (p. 12)

[66] Cf. āhīd-gar-ān below, F 43/4. For a discussion of āhīd see Zaehner; BSOS., IX, 315 sq. Perhaps one can understand Av. āhiti- as "something that causes shame", hence "stain", etc. In that case Anāhitā could be compared to Apsaras. As regards NPers. χīre, mentioned by Zaehner, this may be connected with Sogd. γyr'k "foolish". The word in DkM., 2058, is not necessarily hyrg-gwn (thus Zaehner, ibid., 312). It might be hyl- = Pashto xəṛ "ashen, grey, etc." (p. 12)

[67] Cf. supra, lines 206-212. (p. 12)

[68] On boyuq see Bang, loc. cit., p. 15, who has: "the door of the closed (locked) sun." Acc. to Enoch, chaps. 72 sqq., there are 180 doors in the east one of which is opened each morning for the sun to pass through (the idea, familiar also from Pahlavi books, is of Babylonian origin). (p. 13)

[69] Cf. Enoch, 13, 9, ἦλθον πρὸς αὐτούς, καὶ πάντες συνηγμένοι ἐκάθηντο πενθοῦντες κτλ. (p. 14)

[70] Cf. Enoch, 13, 4-6. (p. 14)

[71] i.e. the divine order for their punishment (Enoch, 10). (p. 14)

[72] [Other fragments of the same manuscript ("T i"), not however belonging to the Kawān, show that there were three columns to a

page; hence, the correct order of the columns is: BCDEFA. Perhaps this text, too, is not a fragment of the Kawān.] (p. 14)

[73] murzīdan is "persecute, harass", not "show pity" as hitherto translated (S 9; Mir.Man., ii; W.-L., ii, 556, r 6). (p. 14)

[74] ghwd (Mir.Man., ii), ghwdg'n (Mir.Man., i), ghwyn- (ZII., ix, 183, 27): the derivation of these words from vi + hū by Schaeder, Sb.P.A.W., 1935, 492, n. 3, is based on the translation I had given; this translation, however, was based on nothing but this selfsame etymology. (p. 14)

[75] Enoch, 10, 10. (p. 15)

[76] This passage in particular seems to show that the text is a fragment of the Kawān. There are two groups of sinners here: one is (apparently) to be transferred from a preliminary fire-prison to the permanent hell at the end of the world (= the Egrēgoroi), the other consists of the κίβδηλοι (= Giants). The digression on their final fate in the great conflagration, under the eyes of the self-satisfied Righteous (cf. Šābuhragān, M 470 V), is well in keeping with Mani's discursive style. (p. 15)

[77] w'y- (different from Parth. w'y- "to lead") = "to fly" or "to hunt" ? Cf. w'ywg "hunter" (BBB., where the translation should be changed), Air. Wb. 1356, 1407. (p. 15)

[78] My pupil I. Gershevitch thinks prβ'r should be derived from prβyr-. It is true that "explanation, announcement" fits most passages better than "chariot"! Hence, Mahāyāna rendered as "the great announcement" ? (p. 15)

[79] Enoch, 17,1: ὅταν θέλωσιν φαίνονται ὡσεὶ ἄνθρωποι. pts'δ, cf. Skt. praticchanda-. (p. 16)

[80] viz. the human associates of the demons, esp. the "daughters of men". (p. 16)

[81] viz. the giants and their children ? Or merely the children of the giants ? See below, S. to Syncellus (apud Fl.-R., p. 25) there were three generations: (1) the giants, (2) the Nephīlīm, their sons, and (3) the Eliud, their grandsons. In the Book of Enoch the giants are killed, or rather incited to kill each other, before the Egrēgoroi are punished (ch. 10). Their spirits shall roam the world, until the day of judgement, as πνεύματα πονηρά (15,8-16,1). (p. 16)

[82] This passage shows that the Sogdian text had been translated from either Middle-Persian or Parthian (MPers. ky myhryzd 'c nwx 'wyš'n r'y wyn'rd bwd, Parthian ky w'd jywndg 'c nwx hwyn wsn'd wyr'št bwd). (p. 16)

[83] 'nδyk probably = skill, art, ability (differently, BBB., p. 105). (p. 16)

[84] See above, A 97. (p. 16)

[85] Fairly cursive, difficult to read. (p. 16)

[86] Probably by assimilation from Šamšai (= Šimšai in Ezra). (p. 16)

[87] See above, G 28-9, and below, text M. According to Enoch, ch. 8, the fallen angels imparted to mankind unholy arts and undesirable knowledge, e.g. astrology, cosmetics, soothsaying, metallurgy, production of weapons, even the art of writing (ch. 69, 9). (p. 17)

[88] Presumably the stellar demons. (p. 17)

[89] Cf. JRAS. 1942, 232 n. 6. (p. 18)

[90] If Mani's famous Ertenk was indeed a picture-book, this Vifrās may well have been the explanatory text published together with it; cf. Polotsky's suggestion, Man. Hom., 18, n. 1, on Mani's εἰκών (but see BBB., pp. 9 sq.). There is no reason for "identifying" the Ertenk with Mani's Evangelion (Schaeder, Gnomon, 9, 347). The fragments of the Vifrās (M 35, M 186, M 205, M 258, M 740, T ii K, T iii D 278) will be published at some other opportunity. (p. 18)

[91] The point is that A eats or kills B, after B had finished C. A man killed his brother over the treaaure, but was killed by a third party, etc. The Great Fire will devour the bodily fire which had swallowed the "exterior fire". Hence, Ohya killed Leviathan, but was killed by Raphael. (p. 19)

[92] St. Wikander, Vayu, i [1941], 166, quotes my article on Enoch, and my paper in ZDMG., 1936, p. 4, and remarks that eigentuemlicherweise I had forgotten Al-Ghaḍanfar's notice on Sām and Narīmān. Less careless readers will find Ghaḍanfar's notice quoted in extenso on the page cited by Wikander. (p. 19)

[93] See above, A 98. (p. 20)

[94] Cf. above. A 105 sqq. (p. 20)

[95] Presumably the number of years supposed to have passed from the time of Enoch to the beginning of the reign of Vištāsp. The date for Enoch was probably calculated with the help of the Jewish world-era, or the mundane era of Alexandria (beginning 5493 B.C.), or by counting backwards from the Deluge. Taking 3237 B.C. (but 3251 B.C. according to the Coptic chronology) as the date of the Deluge (see S. H. Taqizadeh, BSOS., X, 122, under c), and adding 669 (= from Enoch's death to the Deluge according to the Hebrew Genesis), and subtracting the number in our fragment, 3,28[8 ?], from 3,237 + 669 = 3,906, the resulting date, 618 B.C., agrees perfectly with the traditional Zoroastrian date for the beginning of Vištāsp's reign (258 + 30 years before Alexander's conquest of Persia, 330 B.C.; cf. Taqizadeh, ibid., 127 sq.). From this one may infer that the famous date for Zoroaster: "258 years before Alexander" was known to Mani (Nyberg, Rel. Alt. Iran, 32 sqq., thinks it was invented towards the beginning of the fifth century). (p. 20)

[96] The name is possibly to be restored in Türk. Man., iii, p. 39, No. 22, R 5, where wy.t'δlp was read by LeCoq. (p. 20)

[97] In quoting this text in ZDMG., 90, p. 5, I took wyjn for what it seemed to be, viz. Vēžan. But as the appearance of Bēžan in connection with Vištāspa is incomprehensible, I have now restored ['ry']n-wyjn, see above, G 26. (p. 21)

[98] For the spelling, cf. kwdws apud Theodore bar Kōnay. (p. 21)

[99] 'mwst = amwast = believer, faithful (not "sad" !), from hmwd-, Arm. havat-. (p. 21)

[100] Hardly "food" or "banquet" ? Cf. Parth. 'wxrn, etc. Also Budd. Sogd. 'wγr- ('wγ'r-) Impf. w'γr-, Inf. 'wγ'wrt, etc.) "to abandon" (SCE., 562; Dhuta, 41; P2, 97, 219; P 7, 82; etc., appears to be of no use here. (p. 21)

[101] Cf. NPers. ǰehāniyān. (p. 21)

[102] Cf. Vd., ii, 20 ? But the Manich. fragment appears to describe the election of Yima to the sovereignty over the world. (p. 21)

[103] Cf. BSOS., X, 102, n. 4. (p. 21)

[104] šyrn'm is a karmadhāraya, = acclamation(s), cheering, cf. e.g. Rustam frg. (P 13, 5) prw RBkw šyrn'm "with loud cheers"; it should not be confused with the bahuvrīhi šyrn'm'k "well-reputed, famous" (e.g. Reichelt, ii, 68, 9; šyrn'm'y, ibid., 61, 2, cf. BBB., 91, on a 11). But šyrn'm is also "(good) fame", see e.g. V.J., 156, 168, 1139 (p. 21)

www.ingramcontent.com/pod-product-compliance
Lightning Source LLC
Chambersburg PA
CBHW040145260326
41905CB00008B/76